NO SMALL CHANGE

100 YEARS
of Sutton High Street

Compiled by Frank Burgess

Design: Shirley Edwards

London Borough of Sutton Libraries and Arts Services

FOREWORD

Frank Burgess is a chartered municipal engineer by profession and an amateur historian by inclination, as well as being a photographer of merit.

He has happily combined all three talents to unravel the puzzles of the past in Sutton, particularly as they affect road patterns and buildings. For twelve years Frank has delighted audiences throughout the Borough with his slide lectures on different areas of Sutton and Cheam, as they were and as they are now. His careful detective work and explanation has delighted audiences running into thousands in libraries alone. He may well have spoken to an equal number over the years in private talks to local societies.

We are now particularly pleased that he is committing his unique knowledge to paper, and that he has entrusted the library service with the publication. This is his second book, we having published *Old Cheam* in 1978.

The London Borough of Sutton Libraries and Arts Services is indebted to Frank Burgess, and others like him, for their researches and studies into local history, which we in turn have been able to distribute in thousands of copies to people in and outside the Borough—an important and rewarding task that we feel is the duty of every Library Authority.

October 1983

ROY SMITH
BOROUGH LIBRARIAN

First published 1983

London Borough of Sutton Libraries and Arts Services
Central Library, St. Nicholas Way, Sutton, Surrey SM1 1EA
Telephone: 01-661 5050

ISBN 0 907335 09 8

Printed by John Bentley (Printers) Ltd., Todmorden. A member of the Dunn & Wilson Group Ltd.

INTRODUCTION

Since the publication of *Old Cheam* in 1978 I have been asked many times whether I would compile a similar record of change in Sutton and include present-day photographs to help identification of the old ones.

I have not hastened to do this, as over the last five years redevelopment and change has been so extensive that 'present-day' photographs would have been rendered obsolete as soon as they were published. One cannot say even now that the major changes have taken place and that the pace of change has slowed down, but it may not be wise to delay any longer.

This booklet, then, is an attempt to meet the demand. It is a combination of past and present views leavened with some miscellaneous old ones for their interest alone, including one or two once familiar shops, etc., which have since disappeared without trace. The modern photographs (with the exception of the back cover photograph, which was taken in 1978), have all been taken in the last twelve months, as far as possible from the same spot as the earlier photograph. The past and present views are arranged in pairs, with the old view on the left-hand page and the caption referring to both under the modern view. As a whole, the views are presented in sequence as one would encounter them from the railway station to the Green.

The photographs span a period of over a century. It is fortunate for my purpose that Sutton started to develop from a small village street about the same time that the early photographers began their outdoor activities, in the 1850s. The earliest known local photographer was a Mr. Lewis Hind, and a number of his early prints have survived with his trade plates on the back. The cover plate of this booklet is one of his, taken in 1865.

ACKNOWLEDGEMENTS

As in the case of *Old Cheam,* the old photographs are reproduced from the large collection which has been gathered together with the generous help of the many owners of original photographs, postcards and other old prints. Those in the Sutton Libraries' collection are used with the permission of the Borough Librarian, Roy Smith, for which I am most grateful. They were made available to me by the willing and helpful co-operation of June Broughton, Local Studies Librarian, without whose help I would not have undertaken the work.

These are friends and colleagues who are still with us, but I am sure they would agree with me that we are all indebted to the people of the past: firstly the old photographers who took and printed such superb examples of their art; then the owners who have preserved them over the years; and finally the present owners who have made them available to us. To all of these I acknowledge with gratitude my indebtedness. In addition, I also apologise to anyone whose picture I may have used without their specific permission.

Finally, I would like to express my gratitude to the designer, Shirley Edwards, another member of the Libraries' staff, for the pleasing presentation of this book.

F.B.
Milhall, Cheam
1983

4

Sutton Station, (OPPOSITE), built by Messrs. Longley in 1883. The photograph was probably taken about 1920. The station was replaced by the present one in 1928. The feature common to both pictures is the Midland Bank building, previously occupied by Messrs. Bowling, Ironmongers, until they moved to Grove Road in 1926.

Looking south from Sutton Court Road. Wootten Brothers (OPPOSITE) opened their high class draper's shop in 1882, on the corner of Grove Road. The watering cart appears to have passed by shortly before the photograph was taken, having filled up beneath the curved stand-pipe visible on the right in Grove Road. The Wootten block was demolished and replaced by Mitre House in 1932 for International Stores Ltd., occupied by Fads in the modern photograph. The intermediate one-way traffic circuit markings can also be seen.

48866. Sutton, High St. F.F.&Cº

Looking north from Grove Road in 1902 (OPPOSITE), shortly after the London County Bank was built on the corner of Sutton Court Road. It is interesting to note the then fashionable art nouveau decoration on the stonework. Apart from the building on the corner of Grove Road, the main difference in the modern scene is the traffic island regulating the one-way circuit.

In the days of stage-coaches, inns displayed their signs prominently over the centre of the carriageway. Each inn proprietor tried to outdo his near competitors; and bigger and more ornate signs were erected, until the time came when large ones collapsed and the government decreed that no more were to be constructed over the roads. The simple one illustrated here at the Cock Hotel in 1870 was demolished with the old hotel in 1897, and replaced by the sign which still stands today to remind us of the former landmark. When first erected, it stood on the hotel forecourt, but was later moved to the centre of the road, probably in about 1920.

A Francis Frith photograph (OPPOSITE), of the old Cock Hotel, with the Cock 'Tap' on the left, taken in 1890. Seven years later a new hotel was built on the site of the old 'Tap', and the old hotel was demolished and replaced by the building which housed Cedars' first shop, with the Prudential office above. When the 'new' Cock Hotel was demolished in 1961 and London Life House built, Cedars extended into the ground floor, as shown in the modern scene.

The rare old photograph opposite, taken in 1886, shows cottages on the corner of Cheam Road on the site of which Barclays Bank building was erected eight years later for London Provincial Bank Ltd. There are no common features to identify in these two photographs, but the site boundaries can be easily recognised.

48863. Sutton. High St. F.F. & Co.

The view opposite, taken by Frith's in 1903, shows the new Municipal Offices (built in 1900) with the Baptist Church, extreme left, on the corner of Hill Road, next to the old terrace of shops in which Ernest Shinner started his drapery business. The modern view shows the store which has replaced the Municipal Offices, and the pedestrianisation of this portion of the street.

In the left-hand view, taken in 1932, the Baptist Church can be seen more clearly than on page 16, and Mr. Shinner has acquired most of the old terrace and clad it with a white faience façade. In 1934 he acquired the Baptist Church, which was demolished to extend his store. The photograph taken in 1983 shows the completed development. Shinners was renamed Allders in 1979.

Ernest Shinner started business in 1899 in a small way in no. 79 High Street, but by 1928 he had bought up almost the whole of the terrace, and the lower photograph, opposite, shows it before modernisation. It will remind older residents that barely a month went by without Mr. Shinner having a sale under some pretext or another. These 'past and present' photographs show the dramatic change which has taken place in the High Street, particularly in the 1970s.

48862. Sutton, High St FF & Co.

Looking south up the hill from St. Nicholas Road. The photograph opposite was taken in 1902 at 1.20 p.m., according to Shinner's clock, when, it appears, most people were having their siesta. The modern version was taken at 11.30 a.m. *on a Sunday:* conditions have certainly changed. There are a number of features which can be identified as the same in each view, particularly on the left-hand side.

Amos Reynolds first traded as a picture framer and gilder, at 77 High Street in 1873. He moved to these premises, on the corner of Saint Nicholas Road, when he acquired the furnishing and undertaking business of Messrs. Eastern and Truncheon. He traded there until 1979, when Shinners were taken over by Allders, and the corner shop was incorporated into the main store.

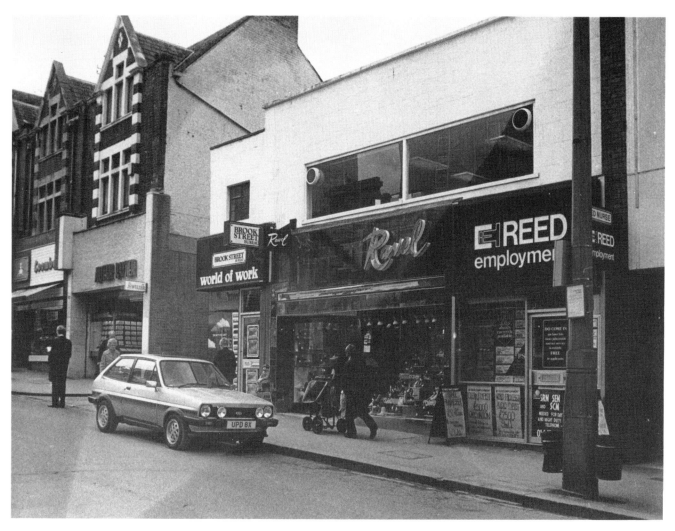

This is a rare case, where there are no remaining features on which to anchor the modern photograph. The exact position of Robert Stevens' little old shop is, however, quite easy to establish from directories, plans, and other photographs, and the modern view shows where it stood. It is also identifiable on the left-hand edge of the next old photograph overleaf.

Leeding's was an old-established firm of coachbuilders which progressed to a modern automobile garage. It ceased business in 1967, when Boots acquired the site and built their modern store. It is worth noting that this store and the new Sainsbury's were the first modern developments to have purpose-built goods access away from the High Street, off the new parallel road, St. Nicholas Way.

The entrance to Messrs. Leeding's yard was where number 113 High Street is today. These two photographs show the transition of their business from carriage builders, established in 1823, to automobile coachbuilders.

Looking down the street (OPPOSITE), about 1880 to the corner of West Street, with the signboard of the Greyhound inn on its beam across the road, beneath which is a flock of sheep on their way to one of the butchers' establishments. On the left can be seen the sign of W. Herrington's pawnbroker's shop, almost opposite which is the white-walled entrance to Tom Pearson's smithy. In the modern photograph that entrance can still be identified, leading to Pearson's cycle workshop.

48888. Sutton High St. F.F. & Co.

34

Opposite is an almost identical location to the previous page, but taken in 1902. The buildings on the left-hand side can be recognised in the modern photograph, and the pillar-box is in both views. This is an unusual box in so far as it bears no royal cipher. It was erected about 1882.

There is little in these two plates common to both, but the locations are in fact precise. The old one (taken about the turn of the century) shows Slate House, a large house which was the residence of a veterinary surgeon. In front of it were the two small shops, one a harness maker's and the other a ham, beef, and meat pie shop called Cheeseman's, which many will remember. The white house beyond, called Garden House, was occupied by a dentist for many years. Next to it was the Greyhound Hotel, on the very edge of the picture.

These two views showing the junction of West Street and High Street can be dated to approximately 1924 and 1932 respectively. They both show the tree, which still remains today, outside the Greyhound Hotel; and the sign on the beam over the highway. This structure remained until 1938, when it was removed to enable the carriageway to be widened.

The photograph opposite is a later view of the Greyhound Hotel. It must have been taken in the mid-1950s, as the concrete lamp column was erected about 1953 and the hotel was demolished in 1959. In the modern view the lamp column is a good anchor point, showing how far Marks & Spencer extended, and the fact that Trueform changed position to a point between Woolworth's and Marks & Spencer's.

This good photograph (OPPOSITE) of the Greyhound Hotel was taken about 1900. The way to the right, beside the hotel, was a public footpath which was originally an ancient field path to Carshalton, and which is still perpetuated in the narrow alley between Trueform's and Marks & Spencer's shops.

These two views from West Street, looking up the hill to the Cock Hotel, are a good indication of the change which has taken place in the street in the past hundred years. The old photograph can be dated between about 1882, when the pillar-box on the left-hand pavement was erected, and 1898, when the old Cock Hotel, visible in the centre of the picture, was demolished.

46

Odd & Sons' sports goods and toy shop was on the corner of West Street. The firm was renowned world-wide for its cricket bats, which they made in a works in West Street from willow grown locally along the Pyl Brook. The price tickets on the bats in the window can be read on the original photograph, and they range from 7/6 to 9/11 (37½p to 50p).

Edward Hawkins' shop at no. 50 High Street was two doors up from Throwley Road; and, apart from the wonderful collection of garden tools and ironmongery, the photograph is interesting because it shows the enormous lanterns which many shops had outside their premises before the days of good street lighting.

The photograph opposite is the most delightful view of the High Street in my whole collection. It was probably taken about 1890, and looks down from the Greyhound Hotel towards Manor Lane (now Lodge Place). The large trees in the middle distance are in the grounds of the Manor House, which were bounded by a high brick wall on the east side of the High Street between Manor Lane and Manor Place.

Yet another pair of photographs showing great change, with only one feature left common to both: that is, the high stepped gable on the right of the picture. In the older view there are two, one of which was demolished and the site on the corner of George Street redeveloped in 1982.

High Street, Sutton.

These views looking up the street from Manor Lane show the different eras of development on each side of the street at this point. The left-hand side which can be seen to be the same today was built in 1910, whilst the right-hand side did not change until 1930.

The view opposite was photographed by Francis Frith in 1891, looking down the street from Manor Lane, and showing clearly the high brick wall of the Manor grounds, which were sold up and developed in 1896. On the opposite side was the well-remembered shop of Frost the chemist, with the conventional three large coloured glass flasks in the window. This is the same portion of the street as shown on the front cover plate of 1865. The three brick cottages on the right of the cover picture have been converted to shops, shown in the centre of this 1891 picture.

These two photographs taken in 1896 and 1983, from just above Benhill Avenue junction, are interesting because, with the notable exception of the Eagle Star building at the bottom of the street, nearly all the other buildings are common to both, and yet the street scene is so very different.

Two views of The Grapes, which was built about 1896. Earlier directories, however, list a Grapes Hotel, but no illustration of it has turned up to date. The photograph opposite is another illustration showing the enormous lanterns which were common before good public street lighting.

To older residents, George Webb the plumber was a household name, but very few would be able to say with conviction where precisely his premises were; or rather, what is on the site now. Although there is no common feature to be seen, the 1983 photograph answers the question!

The South Metropolitan Fire Brigade, No. 4 Station, in No. 3 Edward Terrace! This was a terrace of six shops on the east side of the High Street, stretching upwards from the corner of Marshalls Road, and number 3 is currently number 250 High Street. The two appliances in the left-hand view (OPPOSITE) are horse-drawn manual pumps, which were superseded by the steam pump on the right. Unfortunately, the 'picture' window (ABOVE) has obliterated the three rather ornate original windows on the first floor, but the second floor ones above are recognisable. This greengrocer's open-fronted shop was previously Black's camping shop.

The local lock-up, or 'Cage' as it was familiarly known, stood on the east side of the street approximately opposite Crown Road; but it was too small to be shown distinctly on the Ordnance Survey maps, and consequently its precise position has been lost. The modern photograph, however, shows its general location. The date of the old photograph is not known, but it is amusing to see a 'To let' notice on it, presumably with vacant possession!

It is hardly believable, but the old photograph of wooden cottages converted into shops was taken as recently as about 1930, two years before they were demolished. They stood between George Webb's plumber's yard on the right and Lawson's fish shop (just visible on the left of the picture), on the corner of Elm Grove. It is no coincidence that Camille's Flower House, in the modern photograph, is number 228, but it must be pure chance that the modern lamp standard in the pedestrian precinct is in the same spot as the old one!

These old cottages, which stood on the bend of the High Street, opposite Crown Road, look somewhat strange in the Sutton scene, but they can be located without doubt from the gable of the Red Lion on the right, which can also be seen in the modern view with Tesco's block beyond.

J. W. Lye's premises can only be located with the aid of old street directories and Ordnance Survey maps. These show it to have been opposite Vale Road; and the site is now occupied by the Phoenix Used Car Centre.

The 1896 Frith photograph opposite, looking beyond the High Street, up Angel Hill to the cutting, shows the Cricketers Inn, with All Saints Church towering above it. The modern photograph had to be taken nearer to the Cricketers than the old one was, to enable a sight of half the Church tower to be seen, just to the left of the modern block of Helena House, so that the two photographs could be matched up.

Of all the public houses in the High Street, the Cricketers Inn has changed least in outward appearance. It really needs nothing else to match up the photographs, but nevertheless the tall chimneys on the right put the final seal on it.

'Open all hours'

This most essential item stood on the forecourt of the Cricketers Inn, and was a great 'convenience' to the 'late turn' bus crews, after the modern toilet on the corner of the Green had closed for the night. However, being open-topped, it became a little too 'convenient' to view from the upper windows of the adjacent new tall office block, built in 1962; so it was removed, and is now preserved in an open-air museum in the Midlands.